LOVE
LIKE THAT

Companion Workbook
for Individuals and
Small Groups

LOVE
LIKE THAT

CONTENTS

Leveraging Your
Love Like That Workbook

This is a practical companion guide to *Love Like That*. It will help you apply what you are reading in the book – and make it personal. In other words, this workbook will help you love more like Jesus. Daily.

So, whether you've been walking with Jesus for a long time or you're exploring a new relationship with him, this workbook is for you. And it's ideal for **individual study**.

However, this workbook is also perfect as a **small group guide**. You can use it in a six-session series with others who are reading the book, too. In fact, we have a great video series you may want to use in your group.

The last few pages of this workbook are designed specifically for group use (including an icebreaker for each session, a place to take notes on the video session, group discussion questions, and so on).

Each of the six chapters of this workbook follow the same outline of content in the book, *Love Like That*. So, whether you're doing this on your own or in a group, read the chapter in the book first, then do the related workbook session.

One more thing: make this workbook your own. Mark it up! The more you write in it, the more you'll get out of it.

And let me hear from you.
Send me a note for any reason at:

LesParrott@LoveLikeThatBook.com

Wishing you the very best as you learn to Love Like That,

Les Parrott, Ph.D.
Seattle, Washington

WHY LOVE LIKE JESUS?

BECAUSE THIS IS THE VERY BEST WAY TO LOVE

WHY LOVE LIKE JESUS?

Let's start with the very first paragraph in the book. I don't think I've ever written a more vulnerable piece. But I felt compelled to let you know, right at the top, that I'm far from being a good example of someone who loves like Jesus. How about you?

When it comes to loving like Jesus:

I'm struggling   Got it locked in

1	2	3	4	5	6	7	8	9	10

Why did you rate yourself the way you did?

_____

_____

_____

How's your motivation level for wanting to love like Jesus?

Whatever   Can't be higher

1	2	3	4	5	6	7	8	9	10

Why?

_____

_____

_____

I do my best in the introduction to unpack why loving like Jesus is beyond reason. If you approach it on a purely rational level, you'll say it's impossible. That's why it so often feels out of reach (loving your enemy, walking the extra mile, turning the other cheek).

Of course, this doesn't mean we have to abandon our brain and become deluded to think we can do this. It means **we must also reason with our heart**. Why? Because that's where Jesus does his most powerful work. So, you've got to come to the entire enterprise of loving like Jesus with your whole heart and mind. How are you doing on that front?

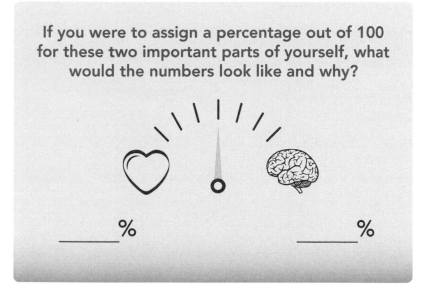

If you were to assign a percentage out of 100 for these two important parts of yourself, what would the numbers look like and why?

_____%   _____%

To love like Jesus, we need to think *and* feel. We need reason and emotion. We need both our head and heart, working together. You'll experience a revolution in your thinking when you allow your heart to enter the conversation. It's what Paul was getting at when he said, "You'll be changed from the inside out" (Romans 12:1-2). What does this mean to you?

_____

_____

_____

As you begin this study on learning to love more like Jesus, what's your biggest fear?

Becoming a doormat?
❑ Yes   ❑ No   Why? _____

Becoming a wimp?
❑ Yes   ❑ No   Why? _____

Giving up fun or pleasure?
❑ Yes   ❑ No   Why? _____

Never getting your own needs met?
❑ Yes   ❑ No   Why? _____

Other fears?

_____

Whatever your fear, I hope to show you in the chapters of this book that they are unwarranted, because loving like Jesus certainly does not mean you'll be getting walked on, that you'll become spineless (far from it!), that you won't have fun (just the opposite), or that your needs will not be met.

The most fulfilled people on the planet are the people who are getting better and better at loving like Jesus. Daily. Why? In part, because they have the healthiest relationships – which is the number one predictor of human happiness.

Think about the happiest, most joyful, and fulfilled people you know. Write their names down (or at least their initials). Are they hedonists? Narcissists? Self-centered? Do they have wealth or fame? Or do they have deep, meaningful, and loving relationships?

_____

_____

_____

As you read through the book you will find that each chapter is a challenge. It calls you to one major task – an **actionable behavior** that is doable once you know what it is and why we tend not to do it. I'm listing them here, and as you read them, give your "blink response" on how much you need what that chapter has to say:

Becoming more mindful - less detached

Not so much   Really need this

| 1 | 2 | 3 | 4 | 5 | 6 | 7 | 8 | 9 | 10 |

Becoming more approachable – less exclusive

Not so much   Really need this

| 1 | 2 | 3 | 4 | 5 | 6 | 7 | 8 | 9 | 10 |

Becoming more grace-full – less judgmental

Not so much   Really need this

| 1 | 2 | 3 | 4 | 5 | 6 | 7 | 8 | 9 | 10 |

Becoming more bold – less fearful

Not so much   Really need this

| 1 | 2 | 3 | 4 | 5 | 6 | 7 | 8 | 9 | 10 |

Becoming more self-giving – less self-absorbed

Not so much   Really need this

| 1 | 2 | 3 | 4 | 5 | 6 | 7 | 8 | 9 | 10 |

Now, review your rankings from the last page. Make a note about why you need each one.

Mindful _____

_____

_____

_____

Approachable _____

_____

_____

_____

Grace-Full _____

_____

_____

_____

Bold _____

_____

_____

_____

Self-Giving _____

_____

_____

_____

One more thing as you are just beginning to read *Love Like That* and use this workbook. It's a suggestion.

Why not take the keystone verse of this book and write it on a card or piece of paper? You can place it somewhere you will see it each day as you are reading the book (perhaps on your mirror or at your desk or kitchen sink). Why? Because it will become a tangible reminder in our journey.

I'm so glad you are doing this study. I can't wait for you to jump into each chapter with me.

Observe how Christ loved us.

His love was not cautious but extravagant.

He didn't love in order to get something from us but to give everything of himself to us.

LOVE LIKE THAT.

– Ephesians 5:2

MINDFUL

SEEING WHAT OTHERS DON'T

1 Think About It

I open the first chapter of *Love Like That* with the story of a brief film that's used in a classic experiment called "Invisible Gorilla." Have you seen it? If not, it's easy to find. Search online and you'll find it and several variations of it within seconds. The video is just a couple of minutes.

As you watch the experiment, consider how susceptible you are to not seeing something that's quite obvious. Would you have seen the gorilla? Why or why not?

Be honest.

_____

_____

_____

_____

2 Getting Personal about Being Mindful

In the book, I say that a mindful person is watchful. They have their eye out for what others are missing. In general, would you say you are more observant or less observant than others?

Example?

_____

_____

_____

_____

I also say that mindfulness means giving others special attention. Who have you given special attention to lately? Can you name someone? What did you do?

Be specific.

_____

_____

_____

_____

A person who is mindful is not detached or oblivious. When do you think you might be most likely to be just that? I realize this could be cringe-worthy, but it's worth noting (if you are feeling brave enough).

_____

_____

_____

_____

What do you fear you are missing out on when it comes to any of your relationships? In other words, what do you fear you are not seeing in some of the people around you?

_____

_____

_____

_____

3 What Keeps You from Being Mindful?

In *Love Like That*, I note that everyone has an agenda – an immediate goal that is continually updated and revised. And it's a powerful force because we are compelled to focus on that goal. Whether it be reading a book, booking a flight, making a call, playing a game, reading a text, or whatever.

If you want to become more mindful, you've got to become more conscious of your agendas. Why? So you can set it aside, temporarily, to focus on someone else and his or her agenda. That's why I want you to consider your most common agendas, be they big or small.

First, list a few people that you think are missing out on loving actions or attitudes from you on occasion because you are consumed with a personal agenda:

Family _____

_____

_____

Friends _____

_____

_____

Coworkers _____

_____

_____

Others _____

_____

_____

Next, list the personal agendas that tend to occupy your mind. Then, note when this tends to happen, and how this agenda keeps you from being more loving and attentive to a specific person in your life.

Agenda #1 _reading emails_

When It's Likely _before dinner_

Who It Impacts _my spouse_

Agenda #2 _____

When It's Likely _____

Who It Impacts _____

Agenda #3 _____

When It's Likely _____

Who It Impacts _____

Agenda #4 _____

When It's Likely _____

Who It Impacts _____

Agenda #5 _____

When It's Likely _____

Who It Impacts _____

Agenda #6 _____

When It's Likely _____

Who It Impacts _____

Of course, there's nothing wrong with having agendas (that's how we get things done). The only problem with them arises when they interfere with our desire to be more loving.

Go back to this list you have generated and lift out a couple that you think you can manage a bit better. Are you game? Think about how your loving actions might be positively impacted if you temporarily set your agenda aside. What will you do to make that happen? Note it here and be as specific as you can.

Item #1 _____

Who It Helps _____

What I Can Change _____

_____

_____

_____

_____

_____

Item #2 _____

Who It Helps _____

What I Can Change _____

_____

_____

_____

_____

_____

Love Like That Workbook

4   How Mindful Are You?

If you haven't done so already, be sure to take the 10-item self-inventory in the chapter. Better yet, do it online at LoveLikeThatBook.com. This takes just a couple of minutes. And if you do it online, you'll appreciate seeing your progress as you move through the other chapters of the book (we give you a nice summary report at the end). So, go ahead. Take the inventory now.

With your results in hand, how do you feel about the percentile score you have? And why?

_____

_____

_____

Are you willing to invite a trusted friend to review the results of your self-inventory? Why or why not?

_____

_____

_____

Mindful

Take the Mindful self-inventory at LoveLikeThatBook.com now. You can save your results and fill out the other sections as you go to complete the picture.

5 Digging into What Jesus Taught

In the book I highlight the story Jesus told about the good Samaritan, one of his most popular parables. It's found in Luke 10:25-37 (NIV):

25 On one occasion an expert in the law stood up to test Jesus. "Teacher," he asked, "what must I do to inherit eternal life?"

26 "What is written in the Law?" he replied. "How do you read it?"

27 He answered, "'Love the Lord your God with all your heart and with all your soul and with all your strength and with all your mind'[a]; and, 'Love your neighbor as yourself.'[b]"

28 "You have answered correctly," Jesus replied. "Do this and you will live."

29 But he wanted to justify himself, so he asked Jesus, "And who is my neighbor?"

30 In reply Jesus said: "A man was going down from Jerusalem to Jericho, when he was attacked by robbers. They stripped him of his clothes, beat him and went away, leaving him half dead. 31 A priest happened to be going down the same road, and when he saw the man, he passed by on the other side. 32 So too, a Levite, when he came to the place and saw him, passed by on the other side. 33 But a Samaritan, as he traveled, came where the man was; and when he saw him, he took pity on him. 34 He went to him and bandaged his wounds, pouring on oil and wine. Then he put the man on his own donkey, brought him to an inn and took care of him. 35 The next day he took out two denarii[c] and gave them to the innkeeper. 'Look after him,' he said, 'and when I return, I will reimburse you for any extra expense you may have.'

36 "Which of these three do you think was a neighbor to the man who fell into the hands of robbers?"

37 The expert in the law replied, "The one who had mercy on him." Jesus told him, "Go and do likewise."

Questions to ponder from the parable:

- The characters in the story include the priest, the Levite, the Samaritan, the man who was beaten. Who might these people be today?
- If you were to project yourself into the story, who would you be? Why?
- What agendas did the various characters in the story have?

_____

_____

_____

_____

6 Getting Real about Being More Mindful

Note the person or persons in your life that you feel need more mindfulness from you. Use their initials if you like and note why you think you need to be more mindful with them.

_____

_____

In the coming week, what is one practical thing you can do, in specific terms, to become more mindful of the people you've just noted? Take time to really ponder this. Be as concrete and specific as you can be. Think not only about what you will do to be more mindful of them, but when you are most likely to do it. And note what is most likely to keep you from actually doing it – and how you won't let it.

_____

_____

APPROACHABLE

MOVING OUT OF YOUR COMFORT ZONE

1 Think About It

Ever felt left out? Snubbed? Silly question, I know. There's not a human alive that hasn't experienced the feeling of being ignored.

As you delve into this topic at a personal level, consider a time that you can still remember– a time when you didn't feel included. Take a note or two on how you felt and what you did. Be as honest with yourself about this feeling as you can. Why? Because the more you understand your own emotional pain in this experience, the more you will be able to understand others and the more approachable you can become.

_____

_____

_____

_____

2 Getting Personal about Being Approachable

In the book, I note a classic study where people would agree that one line is shorter than another line—when it was plainly not—just to fit in with the crowd. How would you have responded in that experiment? Would you have conformed to not be left out or would you have said what you honestly thought? Why or why not?

_____

_____

_____

_____

In the book, I also show how Jesus was tuned in to outcasts, people on the fringes (lepers, Gentiles, tax collectors, the poor, pagans, and sinners). Why do you think he was so intentional (especially in contrast to other teachers in the temple) about being accessible to the undesirable or ignored? If you were a regular temple-attender in those days, how would you have felt about him doing this?

_____

_____

_____

_____

_____

I quote theologian Helmut Thielick: "Jesus was able to love because he loved right through the mud." How do you interpret that? What does he mean? More importantly, what's the "mud" in your life that Jesus loves right through? And is there someone you have a tough time loving because of his or her mud?

_____

_____

_____

_____

One quick and relatively easy way for many of us to become more approachable with others is to simply smile. Studies back this up. So how about you? Do you have an easy smile with others or do you have to work at that? How do you know?

_____

_____

_____

_____

3 | What Keeps You from Being Approachable?

In *Love Like That*, I note that the biggest barrier to being approachable is unhealthy pride. It's what causes us to be exclusive, not inclusive. Pride, the kind that comes from a bloated and insecure ego, makes a mockery of our attempts to include others.

How would you rate your level of unhealthy pride over the past week?

Genuinely humble   Self-consumed
and pretty inclusive   and pretty exclusive

| 1 | 2 | 3 | 4 | 5 | 6 | 7 | 8 | 9 | 10 |

(Note where you fall on this continuum when you were at your best and at your worst over the past seven days.)

Why did you answer the way you did? Give an example of you at your worst on this scale this past week. What happened? Why?

_____

_____

_____

_____

Now give an example of you at your best on this scale this past week. What happened and why?

_____

_____

_____

_____

What can you do, in specific terms, in the upcoming week to set your unhealthy pride aside so that you can be more inclusive of those who may be feeling marginalized? Is there a particular person you want to focus on? A time and a place?

_____

_____

_____

4 How Approachable Are You?

Just as you did in the previous chapter, be sure to take the 10-item self-inventory at LoveLikeThatBook.com. How do you feel about the percentile score you have? And why?

_____

_____

_____

_____

Are you willing to invite a trusted friend to review the results of your self-inventory? If so, what are you learning from their input?

_____

_____

_____

_____

5 | What Jesus Taught about Being Approachable

In the book I highlight the story Jesus told to demonstrate the irony of pride and humility in our lives. He told it to people who were particularly pleased with themselves. It's found in Luke 18:9-14 (NIV):

> [9] To some who were confident of their own righteousness and looked down on everyone else, Jesus told this parable: [10] "Two men went up to the temple to pray, one a Pharisee and the other a tax collector. [11] The Pharisee stood by himself and prayed: 'God, I thank you that I am not like other people—robbers, evildoers, adulterers—or even like this tax collector. [12] I fast twice a week and give a tenth of all I get.'
>
> [13] "But the tax collector stood at a distance. He would not even look up to heaven, but beat his breast and said, 'God, have mercy on me, a sinner.'
>
> [14] "I tell you that this man, rather than the other, went home justified before God. For all those who exalt themselves will be humbled, and those who humble themselves will be exalted."

Questions to ponder from the parable:

- Jesus is calling us to humble ourselves. How are you doing that? Are you at any risk of being proud of how humble you are?

- Do you ever look at other people who don't believe or act the way you do (maybe they don't attend church, for example) and think you're better than they are? Why or why not?

_____

_____

_____

_____

6 Getting Real about Being More Approachable

Who in your life would you like to be more approachable with? It could be specific people or a group of people. Use their initials if you like and note why.

_____

_____

_____

_____

In the coming week, what is one practical thing you can do, in specific terms, to become more approachable with the people you've just noted? Take time to really ponder this. Be as concrete and specific as you can. Think not only about what you will do to be more approachable, but when you are most likely to do it. And note what is most likely to keep you from actually doing it – and how you won't let it.

_____

_____

_____

_____

Approachable

Take the Approachable self-inventory at LoveLikeThatBook.com now. You can save your results and fill out the other sections as you go to complete the picture.

GRACE-FULL

LOVING PEOPLE WHO DON'T DESERVE IT

LOVE
LIKE THAT

1 Think About It

Okay. Here's a soul-searching question that you probably don't have to ponder too long. To get your wheels turning as you get into this topic, answer this: When have you most needed grace? What was the catalyst or cause for your need of grace and who, if anyone, gave it to you? Note whatever comes to mind – be it big or small.

To take the question to an even more personal level, let me ask: Are you currently needing a grace-gift from yourself? In other words, are you needing to give grace to you for something you continue to punish yourself for? Are you carrying a bag of guilt when God has already forgiven you?

As you prime the pump for this important study of this chapter, I want to be sure you make it personal. Why? Because the more in touch you are with your need of grace, the more likely you are to learn how you can better offer it to others.

_____

_____

_____

_____

2 Getting Personal about Being Grace-Full

In the book, I talk about an experience I had in graduate school where I was taught about "unconditional positive regard" – a clinical practice for offering grace and acceptance to others. The idea is to help others drop their pretenses in the context of being fully known and valued by another person. When was the last time you were intentional about offering this kind of powerful acceptance to someone? Why did you offer it? How difficult was it? What was the result?

_____

_____

_____

_____

Mercy is getting spared from bad things you deserve. Grace is getting good things you don't deserve. Which one comes easier for you to offer others and why?

_____

_____

_____

_____

Who in your life most needs a grace-gift from you and why?

_____

_____

_____

_____

3   What Keeps You from Being Grace-Full?

In _Love Like That_, I note we call on judgmentalism whenever we feel insecure. It puffs us up, feeding our self-deception, telling us we are superior. We tear others down to build ourselves up.

Think through your interactions and attitudes toward others. How judgmental would you say you've been over the past few days? Take some time to really ponder this before you answer.

How judgmental would you say you've been over the past few days?

Grace-Full   Judgmental
to a fault   by reflex

| 1 | 2 | 3 | 4 | 5 | 6 | 7 | 8 | 9 | 10 |

(Note where you fall on this continuum when you were at your best and at your worst over the past seven days.)

Why did you answer the way you did? Give an example of you at your worst on this scale over the past few days. What happened? Why?

_____

_____

_____

Now give an example of you at your best on this scale this past week. What happened? Who did you give grace to and why?

_____

_____

_____

What can you do, in specific terms, in the upcoming week to set your insecure delusion of superiority aside so that you can be more grace-full to those who you can love even when they don't deserve it? Is there a particular person you want to focus on? A time and a place?

_____

_____

_____

4 How Grace-Full Are You?

Just as you did in the previous chapters, be sure to take the 10-item self-inventory at LoveLikeThatBook.com. How do you feel about the percentile score you have? And why?

_____

_____

_____

Are you willing to invite a trusted friend to review the results of your self-inventory? If so, what are you learning from their input?

_____

_____

_____

5 What Jesus Taught about Being Grace-Full

In the book I highlight the story Jesus told to his disciple, Peter, when he was asking Jesus a pretty straight forward question: "We left everything and followed you. What do we get out of it?" The parable Jesus gave him in answer to his question caught him off guard. It's found in Matthew 20:8-15 (NIV):

> 8 "When evening came, the owner of the vineyard said to his foreman, 'Call the workers and pay them their wages, beginning with the last ones hired and going on to the first.'
> 9 "The workers who were hired about five in the afternoon came and each received a denarius. 10 So when those came who were hired first, they expected to receive more. But each one of them also received a denarius. 11 When they received it, they began to grumble against the landowner. 12 'These who were hired last worked only one hour,' they said, 'and you have made them equal to us who have borne the burden of the work and the heat of the day.'
> 13 "But he answered one of them, 'I am not being unfair to you, friend. Didn't you agree to work for a denarius? 14 Take your pay and go. I want to give the one who was hired last the same as I gave you. 15 Don't I have the right to do what I want with my own money? Or are you envious because I am generous?'

Questions to ponder from the parable:

- You have to admit, Jesus is being pretty unconventional here, right? If Peter was looking for a benefit plan in this parable, he didn't find the one he was expecting. How about you? How would you feel if you were in Peter's shoes, walking with Jesus and asking him about the benefits of being his disciple?

- The Grace-Giver from Nazareth doesn't work according to a tiered system of reward. That's not how his vineyard operates. How does that make you feel? Are you glad or a little miffed because it doesn't seem fair to have a grace-filled vineyard where the first are last and the last are first? Why?

_____

_____

_____

_____

_____

6 Getting Real about Being More Grace-Full

Who in your life would you like to be more grace-full with? It could be specific people or a group of people. Use their initials if you like and note why.

_____

_____

_____

_____

In the coming week, what is one practical thing you can do, in specific terms, to become more grace-full with the people you've just noted? Take time to really ponder this. Be as concrete and specific as you can be. Think not only about what you will do to be more grace-full, but when you are most likely to do it. And note what is most likely to keep you from actually doing it – and how you won't let it.

_____

_____

_____

_____

Grace-Full

Take the Grace-Full self-inventory at LoveLikeThatBook.com now. You can save your results and fill out the other sections as you go to complete the picture.

SESSION 5

BOLD

SPEAKING TRUTHFULLY
AND RISKING REJECTION

1 Think About It

Early into this chapter of the book I note the fabled story by Hans Christian Anderson of "The Emperor's New Clothes." Here's my question for you: If you were one of the villagers, would you have gone along with the crowd, believing that the naked emperor was wearing glorious clothing?

As you delve into this topic at a personal level, consider a time when you didn't speak up when you know you should have. It may have been for yourself or for someone else. It may have been long ago or just this week. What kept you from being bolder in that situation?

_____

_____

_____

_____

2 Getting Personal about Being Bold

In the book, I note that an almost startling quality of Jesus is his unswerving authenticity. He never seemed to shy away from many showdowns. He didn't dance around what needed to be said. He was a straight shooter.

How about you? Would the people who know you best – when they are talking about you amongst themselves – describe you as authentic? Would they say you speak up for what you know to be right and true, even if it means you might not be welcomed? Would they say you're fearless when it comes to being truthful? Why or why not?

_____

_____

_____

_____

Love Like That Workbook

In the book, I also note that Jesus never allowed truth to take a back seat to politeness. And the group he confronted most was the group that he most resembled. Scholars agree that Jesus, the rabbi from Nazareth, most closely matched the profile of a Pharisee. Yet Jesus singled out the Pharisees more than any other group for his strongest critiques. He boldly called them hypocrites (see Matthew 23:23-24). Why do you think he did this?

_____

_____

_____

How would you have felt if you were a Pharisee in the time of Christ? It's easy to cheer Jesus on in his bold confrontations with this "brood of vipers." But what if you were one of them? Or maybe a better question is, how are you like them today? He seemed to be most disturbed that they were focused on externals rather than the internals of their faith. He called them out for be legalistic and pointed out that they were focused more on impressing others than loving God. Does that critique hit anywhere close to home for you? Why or why not? And how might it impede your inclination to be bold, authentic, and congruent in your faith?

_____

_____

_____

3   What Keeps You from Being a Bold Truth-Teller?

In *Love Like That*, I write that the biggest barrier to being bold is our fear of rejection. We're afraid of being alienated or losing approval and acceptance. So, we wear masks. We act indifferent when something truly irks us. We clam up when we really have something to say. We vacillate between the impulse to reveal ourselves and the impulse to protect ourselves. What interpersonal masks do you tend to wear, and where do you tend to wear them most (home, work, etc.)?

_____

_____

_____

If you were to draw a common mask you wear, how would you depict it? Don't worry about your sketching skills, just draw what you think represents one or two of your interpersonal masks.

If we wear our masks long enough, we become perpetually weak and incongruent (not bold). And that keeps us from ever really loving like Jesus. Knowing that it can mean risking rejection, what can you do to take off your masks and be more authentic? In practical terms, what would a particular relationship or situation look like if you slipped off your mask to boldly say what needed to be said?

_____

_____

_____

_____

_____

4 | How Bold Are You?

Just as you did in the previous chapters, be sure to take the 10-item self-inventory at LoveLikeThatBook.com. How do you feel about the percentile score you have? And why?

_____

_____

_____

_____

Are you willing to invite a trusted friend to review the results of your self-inventory? If so, what are you learning from their input?

_____

_____

_____

_____

5 | What Jesus Taught about Being Bold

In the book I highlight a teaching Jesus gave in his Sermon on the Mount. He is calling us to quit playing games and be authentic and congruent with our lives. His straight-shooting words are found in Matthew 5:33-37 (MSG):

> 33-37 "And don't say anything you don't mean. This counsel is embedded deep in our traditions. You only make things worse when you lay down a smoke screen of pious talk, saying, 'I'll pray for you,' and never doing it, or saying, 'God be with you,' and not meaning it. You don't make your words true by embellishing them with religious lace. In making your speech sound more religious, it becomes less true. Just say 'yes' and 'no.' When you manipulate words to get your own way, you go wrong.

Questions to ponder from the parable:

- As I say in the book, truth without love is ugly, and love without truth is spineless. How are you doing when it comes to being bold with your truth and speaking it when you should? Do you agree with Jesus when he makes the point that you're only making things worse when you "lay down a smokescreen of pious talk?" What would be an example of that in your own life?

- What about the "religious lace" Jesus talks about? Can you think of a time when you tended to speak religious words just out of habit but not out of the heart?

_____

_____

_____

_____

_____

_____

6 Getting Real about Being More Bold

Who in your life would you like to be bolder with? It could be specific people or a group of people. Use their initials if you like and note why.

_____

_____

_____

_____

In the coming week, what is one practical thing you can do, in specific terms, to become bolder with the people you've just noted? Take time to really ponder this. Be as concrete and specific as you can be. Think not only about what you will do to be bolder, but when you are most likely to do it. And note what is most likely to keep you from actually doing it – and how you won't let it.

_____

_____

_____

_____

Bold

Take the Bold self-inventory at LoveLikeThatBook.com now. You can save your results and fill out the other sections as you go to complete the picture.

SELF-GIVING

EMPTYING YOURSELF FOR EMPATHY

1 Think About It

Think back on your childhood. Can you recall a time when you were particularly selfish—a time when you almost literally felt that the world revolved around you? It's not unusual. As children, we were all self-absorbed. It was essential to our survival in some ways. Learning the ins and outs of this big world can cause a lot of anxiety and fear. So, we focus on ourselves. We become unabashedly selfish (with food, toys, time, desires, whatever).

But as we mature, of course, we grow out of that. Or do we? Can you think of a time as an adult where you were almost just as consumed with your own needs as you were when you were a child? A time you felt entitled, like everyone owed you? You might be cringing, like I am. But that's okay. It's important to be honest about our selfish ways. If we don't own them, we won't move beyond them.

_____

_____

_____

_____

2 Getting Personal about Being Self-Giving

In the book, I note a paradox: Selfish people are, by definition, those whose activities are devoted to bringing themselves happiness. Yet, these selfish people are far less likely to be happy than those whose efforts are devoted to making others happy. What do you make of that? In fact, when do you see yourself as being most selfish (be specific about what you do and when you tend to do it). What's the emotional result for you?

_____

_____

_____

_____

Love Like That Workbook

Jesus says something time and again in his teachings: "Whoever finds his life will lose it, and whoever loses his life for my sake will find it." He flips our intuitive sense of self-interest inside out. Right? Do you agree with his point? Why or why not?

_____

_____

_____

_____

More importantly, how do you think you're doing at putting this into practice?

I've got a lock on
being self-giving

I'm a long way from
being selfless

1	2	3	4	5	6	7	8	9	10

As you review your past week or so, would you say you are about as selfish as the average person? More? Less? Most people say they are less self-centered than the average person. In other words, most of us think we are "above average" when it comes to being self-giving. Do you? Why or why not?

_____

_____

_____

_____

3   What Keeps You from Being Self-Giving?

The greatest barrier to compassion and self-giving is fear. We fear not being first or not getting what we need or want. So, we seek our own advantage and look past what might be helpful to others. What would those who know you best say about your inclination to routinely put others' needs ahead of your own?

_____

_____

_____

_____

When it comes to transcending the fear of not getting what you want or need (whether it's tangible or emotional), what would you say – in specific terms – is keeping you from being more self-giving? Can you name the fear or at least describe it in more detail for yourself?

_____

_____

_____

_____

What will help you break the instinctual habit of routinely putting your own interests first? Jesus gives a clear-cut path for doing just that ("going the extra mile," as you know from reading this chapter of _Love Like That_). Does it scare you like it does me? Why? Consider three or four important relationships in your life right now. What would it look like to walk the extra mile in each of them? Be as specific and concrete as you can.

_____

_____

_____

_____

To follow up on this previous question, what can you do, in specific terms, in the upcoming week to set aside your fear of "missing out" so that you can be more self-giving to those around you? Is there a particular person you most want to focus on? A time and a place?

_____

_____

_____

_____

4 How Self-Giving Are You?

Just as you did in the previous chapters, be sure to take the 10-item self-inventory at LoveLikeThatBook.com. This time you will not only receive information on this subscale of being self-giving, but you will receive an overall average score on all five scales together. How do you feel about the percentile score you have? And why?

_____

_____

_____

_____

Are you willing to invite a trusted friend to review the results of your self-inventory – including your overall score? If so, what are you learning from their input?

_____

_____

_____

_____

5   What Jesus Taught about Being Self-Giving

In the book I highlight the greatest relationship lesson ever taught, the greatest sermon ever preached. Jesus preached his sermon to a crowd overlooking the Sea of Galilee. And it was revolutionary. The whole sermon is found in Matthew 5 through 7. But here is just a portion from near the beginning of his teaching and, as in the book, I want to draw your attention particularly to the piece where Jesus urged his listeners to walk the extra mile. The fuller context is here in Matthew 5:38-48 (NIV):

> [38] "You have heard that it was said, 'Eye for eye, and tooth for tooth.'[a] [39] But I tell you, do not resist an evil person. If anyone slaps you on the right cheek, turn to them the other cheek also. [40] And if anyone wants to sue you and take your shirt, hand over your coat as well. [41] If anyone forces you to go one mile, go with them two miles. [42] Give to the one who asks you, and do not turn away from the one who wants to borrow from you.
>
> [43] "You have heard that it was said, 'Love your neighbor[b] and hate your enemy.'[44] But I tell you, love your enemies and pray for those who persecute you, [45] that you may be children of your Father in heaven. He causes his sun to rise on the evil and the good, and sends rain on the righteous and the unrighteous. [46] If you love those who love you, what reward will you get? Are not even the tax collectors doing that? [47] And if you greet only your own people, what are you doing more than others? Do not even pagans do that? [48] Be perfect, therefore, as your heavenly Father is perfect.

Questions to ponder from the parable:

- Looking specifically at verses 38-42, in what ways does Jesus' teaching align with or stand in opposition to culture? What would be a practical example of this practice in your own life?

- When you consider this revolutionary message and what Jesus is asking, what is your natural response? What is most likely to keep you from putting it into practice in your own life and why?

_____

_____

_____

6 Getting Real about Being More Self-Giving

Who in your life would you like to be more self-giving with? It could be specific people or a group of people. Use their initials if you like and note why.

_____

_____

_____

In the coming week, what is one practical thing you can do, in specific terms, to become more self-giving with the people you've just noted? Take time to really ponder this. Be as concrete and specific as you can be. Think not only about what you will do to be more self-giving, but when you are most likely to do it. And note what is most likely to keep you from actually doing it – and how you won't let it.

_____

_____

_____

SMALL GROUP GUIDE

WITH ACCOMPANYING VIDEO

This section of the Love Like That Workbook is dedicated to exploring the content of the book together with people who, like you, are invested in loving more like Jesus. And a small group study is probably the best way to explore this content. Why? Because we typically learn more with others – talking things through – than we do on our own.

If you're not in a small group, start one. It's easy. Just invite some people you know to join you for six weeks. Each of you commits to reading the book and meeting for an hour or so once a week to debrief and process what you're reading about. You don't need to be the "leader," either. Just walk through the content of this small group guide. It's as simple as that.

The video series for this group study is available at *RightNowMedia.com*.

One more thing. A key ingredient to a successful group study like this is authenticity. In other words, the benefit of your sessions is directly proportional to how real you are with your fellow group members. So do your best to be transparent and even vulnerable when you can. The more open people are in the group, the more meaningful your sessions will be.

LOVE
LIKE THAT

▶ SESSION 1: MINDFUL

Breaking the Ice *(5 minutes)*

If you've watched the "invisible gorilla" video online (it's easy to find), what was your reaction and why?

Or, if you prefer a different ice breaker: Ever experienced the phenomenon of inadvertently ignoring otherwise obvious navigation tools at the top of a web page? It happens so often it's got a name: Navigational Blindness. What other things are we sometimes blind to?

Video Notes *(15 minutes)*

_____

_____

_____

_____

_____

Talking Through Your Self-Inventory *(10 minutes)*

Okay, this can be a little scary, but if you're willing, share your results of the inventory (what percentage you got) with your group. Talk about how you feel about your score. The more authentic you are, the better. But if you're not feeling up to it, you can always say "I pass," and you don't have to suffer a moment of guilt about it. Regardless, you can take a few notes here:

_____

_____

_____

By the way, if you haven't yet taken the self-inventory on being mindful, you can do it in less than five minutes at LoveLikeThatBook.com.

Discussion Questions *(25 minutes)*

- How did you feel after reading this first chapter of the book?

- Do you agree that we humans can often be astonishingly prone to missing what should be abundantly obvious? Why or why not? Can you identify a specific time when you were "perceptually blind" to something in plain sight?

- How do you relate to Zacchaeus? What kinds of feelings would you have had toward him if you were standing nearby and observing Jesus wanting to visit with this man so many despised? How would you have felt in the moment? Why?

- How does your personal agenda—your immediate goal—keep you from recognizing other people's needs around you? Are you motivated to be more mindful of your own agenda to better love others?

- In reading about Jesus teaching on the good Samaritan, can you imagine what you would have been thinking if you were there, in person, listening to these words? How would you have processed this idea of what we might call a "good Nazi" today?

- How would you rate your current capacity to set your own agenda aside to more clearly see other people and ways to better love them? Are you now more inclined to ask God for wisdom in doing just that? Why or why not?

Prayer (5 minutes)

Lord, help us see what we don't. Open our eyes to the needs around us – especially in the relationships that matter most. Help us become more and more attuned to your spirit so that we look at others through your eyes and see them as you do. Amen.

Breaking the Ice *(5 minutes)*

When you think of a high-profile person who is highly non-approachable, who comes to mind and why? How about the opposite? Who is one of the most approachable people you know (and why)?

Video Notes *(15 minutes)*

_____

_____

_____

_____

_____

_____

Talking Through Your Self-Inventory *(10 minutes)*

After the last session, you know the drill here. If you're willing, share your results of the inventory (what percentage you got) with your group. Talk about how you feel about your score. The more authentic you are, the better. Feel free to write notes:

_____

_____

_____

_____

By the way, if you haven't yet taken the self-inventory on being approachable, you can do it in less than five minutes at LoveLikeThatBook.com.

Discussion Questions *(25 minutes)*

- How did you feel after reading this chapter of the book?

- How would you respond if you were in the experiment where everyone else voted incorrectly for the longest of three lines? Would you stick with your convictions about what you know to be true or give in to be accepted? Why or why not?

- How do you relate to Simon? If you were invited to his dinner party with Jesus, would you have understood and even sided with Simon's attempt to trap this radical person named Jesus who was stirring up so much controversy in your temple? Or would you have been embarrassed by Simon's questions? Why?

- Jesus was incredibly inclusive of those who were rejected by most, the riffraff fringe who were rarely included by others. What about you? Do you want to have a reputation for including those who aren't typically included?

- In reading about Jesus' teaching on the prodigal son, do you identify more with the son or the father and why? In either case, what would you be thinking and feeling?

- How would you rate your current capacity to set your pride aside to be more approachable? Are you being intentional about not sizing others up by their outward appearance, so you can have a welcoming spirit that makes them feel included? Why or why not?

Prayer (5 minutes)

Lord, help us to let down our guard with others and become more accessible and approachable. Just as Jesus invited the little children to him, help us to receive people around us with an open spirit. Just as Jesus was warm and inviting to the outcasts and sinners, help us to be accepting of those that others might reject. Like Jesus, help us to give more weight to our relationships than we do to rules. Help us become more approachable and less exclusive. Amen.

Breaking the Ice *(5 minutes)*

When do you feel most judged by others and why? Or, if you prefer, when do you tend to be most judgmental of others and why?

Video Notes *(15 minutes)*

_____

_____

_____

_____

_____

_____

Talking Through Your Self-Inventory *(10 minutes)*

By this time in your group, you're in a groove. So, why not share your results of the inventory (what percentage you got) with the other members of the group? Talk about how you feel about your score. The more authentic you are, the better. Feel free to write notes:

_____

_____

_____

_____

By the way, if you haven't yet taken the self-inventory on being grace-full, you can do it in less than five minutes at LoveLikeThatBook.com.

Discussion Questions *(25 minutes)*

- How did you feel after reading this chapter of the book?

- What do you make of the sentiment that says mercy is getting spared from bad things you deserve, and grace is getting good things you don't deserve? Do you agree? Why or why not?

- Put yourself in the temple classroom where Jesus was teaching when the religious leaders brought in a woman caught in adultery. Can you imagine? What would be going through your mind as they put Jesus on the spot? Would you have agreed with the grace-giving response of Jesus to this woman?

- Do you think you are above average when it comes to being nonjudgmental? Most people think they are more grace-giving than they actually are. Why is that? And what can you do, in practical terms, to keep your own judgmentalism in view?

- In this grace-filled vineyard that Jesus described in a parable to Peter and the other disciples, he said the first are last and the last are first. How does that sit with you? Be honest. Does it rub you the wrong way? What is the main lesson of this parable for you personally?

- Chances are that you believe God loves you. Right? But when it comes down to it, are you like most others who continue to really think you have to earn God's love? In what ways do you fall for this biblical misnomer? And do you believe that receiving God's unconditional love on a personal level becomes the fuel for loving others unconditionally?

Prayer (5 minutes)

Lord, help us become less judgmental, less critical. Help us to learn your unforced rhythms of grace. Help us to wrap our relationships in acceptance. Help us to offer grace to the people in our lives even when we feel like they don't deserve it. Amen.

▶ SESSION 4: BOLD

Breaking the Ice *(5 minutes)*

Can you think of a time, even from your younger days, when you were more concerned with being accepted or popular than you were with being authentic or honest? What did you do? How did it make you feel?

Video Notes *(15 minutes)*

_____

_____

_____

_____

_____

_____

Talking Through Your Self-Inventory *(10 minutes)*

It's that time again. Share your results of the inventory (what percentage you got) with the other members of the group. Talk about how you feel about your score. The more authentic you are, the better. Feel free to write notes:

_____

_____

_____

_____

By the way, if you haven't yet taken the self-inventory on being bold, you can do it in less than five minutes at LoveLikeThatBook.com.

Discussion Questions *(25 minutes)*

• How did you feel after reading this chapter of the book?

• One of the most compelling stories in the New Testament occurs when Jesus becomes angry in the temple. What do you make of it after reading this chapter? What was his motive, and why did he become so emotional?

• We all fear rejection at some level. That's why we wear interpersonal masks (presenting an image that's not congruent with how we really are). What's your go-to mask when you shy away from truth-telling? Do you wear the "pleasant" mask? The "brush it off with humor" mask? What's your inclination?

• Jesus says we need to speak the truth, but with love: "Confront him with the need for repentance, and offer again God's forgiving love" (Matt 18:17). How have you done this in your own relationships? What's your biggest personal challenge in doing so?

• To be a better truth-teller, a bold person in your relationships, you have to be willing to risk rejection. How would you rate yourself on this ability? What's one practical way for you to improve in this area? Is there a relationship right now that needs your attention in this way?

Prayer (5 minutes)

Lord, give us the strength to seek truth and call it out in a way that honors you. Help us start with ourselves, inviting feedback with an open heart and mind. We want to be authentic and congruent. So help us own those parts of ourselves we'd rather not see. And as we become more honest with ourselves, we want to become better truth-tellers in our lives, not shying away from difficult conversations. Help us to do all this in love. Amen.

Breaking the Ice *(5 minutes)*

In your daily life, when are you at your most selfish? Be honest. When are you most likely to put your own needs and desires above everyone else? And when are you most likely to be self-giving? What makes the difference?

Video Notes *(15 minutes)*

_____

_____

_____

_____

_____

_____

Talking Through Your Self-Inventory *(10 minutes)*

In this last session, once more, share your results of the inventory (what percentage you got) with the other members of the group. Talk about how you feel about your score. And as you know, the more authentic you are, the better. Feel free to write notes:

_____

_____

_____

_____

_____

_____

Discussion Questions *(25 minutes)*

- How did you feel after reading this chapter of the book?

- What do you make of the survey showing that only 17 percent of us say we are selfish, but we see most other people as being selfish most of the time? Do you admit you are a selfish person at least some of the time? Why or why not? Are you more self-focused or less self-focused than most other people you know?

- Imagine being in the upper room with Jesus and the disciples for the last supper. Jesus, your teacher, begins to carefully wash your feet with water. Put yourself in that day and age with all the meaning this custom would have. How are you feeling and why? What "flashbulb memory" would you take with you from that experience?

- Do you agree that the greatest barrier to compassion is fear - the fear of not being first, of not getting what you want? Can you recount a concrete example of this from your own life? What does it teach you?

- When Jesus taught the principle of going the extra mile it was – and still is – radical. Do you aspire to do that in your relationships? Why or why not? When was the last time you were intentional about walking the extra mile for someone? What happened?

- How are you doing when it comes to putting yourself in other people's shoes? Would you give yourself good marks for empathy? Why? Can you think of a specific example from the past week where you were intentional about seeing the world – or at least a particular issue – from someone else's perspective?

Prayer (5 minutes)

Lord, one of the greatest human challenges we have is to put our pride and self-centeredness aside to better love others. So, we ask you to help us. Fill us with your Spirit and help us put ourselves in other people's shoes. Most of all, as we wrap up this series together, we ask that we would embrace your love for us so that we might love more and more like Jesus. Amen.

Breaking the Ice *(5 minutes)*

What comes to mind when you think of the Holy Spirit? How conscious are you of the Holy Spirit in a typical week? How would you describe your relationship with the Spirit?

Video Notes *(15 minutes)*

_____

_____

_____

_____

_____

_____

_____

_____

_____

_____

_____

_____

_____

In this final session, reveal your average score across the five sub-scales:

Mindful ☐

Approachable ☐

Grace-Full ☐

Bold ☐

Self-Giving ☐

My Average Score ☐

Talk for a moment about your motivation to work on each one. Which one gets priority from you going forward? Why? Are you intending to come back and take the self-inventories in a month or so to mark your growth in these areas? Feel free to write notes:

_____

_____

_____

_____

_____

_____

Discussion Questions *(25 minutes)*

- How did you feel after reading this chapter of the book?

- Taking a cue from the opening story in this chapter, who has messed up the trajectory of your life? How do your current feelings about this person jive with 1 John 4:20? Can you love this person like Jesus loves them? Why or why not?

- As you review the five concrete ways to love more like Jesus, which one is toughest for you and why?

- The apostle Paul confesses his struggle to love like Jesus and eventually writes about it to the Galatians (see 2:19-21). How much do you identify with what he wrote and why? How would you have felt if you had received this letter from him?

- The chapter notes several names that Scripture gives to the Holy Spirit. Which name do you identify with most and why?

- What did you learn in this chapter about how the Holy Spirit can work in your life to help you love more like Jesus?

Prayer (5 minutes)

Lord, we ask for your Holy Spirit to permeate our lives. Make us more conscious of the work the Spirit is doing and can be doing in our daily lives. When it feels like we can't love someone the way you do, help us to ask for help. Give us sensitive ears to hear the nudgings of the Spirit. Amen.

LOVE LIKE THAT
FOR YOUR CHURCH

Guide your congregation through a **six-week series** that will revolutionize relationships.

This **turn-key kit** includes everything you need for compelling sermons and life-changing small groups based on the new book by bestselling author and ordained minister **Dr. Les Parrott.**

LoveLikeThatBook.com